Adjectives

big

rough

green

huge

by Josh Gregory

CHERRY LAKE PUBLISHING · ANN ARBOR, MICHIGAN

CHERRY
LAKE
Publishing

A note on the text: Certain words are highlighted as examples of adjectives.

Bold, colorful words are vocabulary words and can be found in the glossary.

Published in the United States of America by Cherry Lake Publishing
Ann Arbor, Michigan
www.cherrylakepublishing.com

Content Adviser: Lori Helman, PhD, Associate Professor, Department of Curriculum & Instruction, University of Minnesota, Minneapolis, Minnesota

Photo Credits: Page 4, ©Tomasz Bidermann/Shutterstock.com; page 8, ©Charlotte Leaper/Dreamstime.com; page 14, ©Kjersti Joergensen/Shutterstock, Inc.; page 15, ©Tatiana Morozova/Shutterstock, Inc.; page 17, ©apiguide/Shutterstock, Inc.; page 20, ©Yuri Arcurs/Shutterstock, Inc.

Library of Congress Cataloging-in-Publication Data
Gregory, Josh.
  Adjectives / By Josh Gregory.
     pages cm. — (Language Arts Explorer Junior) (Basic tools) (21st Century Junior Library)
  Includes bibliographical references and index.
  ISBN 978-1-62431-180-2 (lib. bdg.) — ISBN 978-1-62431-246-5 (e-book) — ISBN 978-1-62431-312-7 (pbk.)
1. English language—Adjective—Juvenile literature. 2. English language—Grammar—Juvenile literature. I. Title.

PE1241.G58 2013
428.2—dc23   2013006653

Cherry Lake Publishing would like to acknowledge the work of The Partnership for 21st Century Skills. Please visit www.p21.org for more information.

Printed in the United States of America
Corporate Graphics Inc.
July 2013
CLFA13

Table of Contents

CHAPTER ONE
At the Zoo 4

CHAPTER TWO
Comparing Things 10

CHAPTER THREE
Other Types of Adjectives 14

Glossary 22
For More Information 23
Index 24
About the Author 24

At the Zoo

There are many wonderful things to see at the zoo.

Tom and his sister, Kate, were so excited. They could barely keep from yelling as they neared the ticket booth. Their Uncle Mike was taking them to the zoo. Neither of them had ever been to the zoo before. They were looking forward to seeing all kinds of animals.

What do you imagine when Kate describes the bush outside the zoo?

"Look at that huge bush!" Tom shouted in surprise. He pointed to a bush that had been trimmed to look like one of the animals in the zoo.

"That is awesome," Kate said. "It looks just like a big, green elephant."

"What animals are you guys most excited to see?" asked Uncle Mike.

"I can't wait to see the beautiful birds and the silly monkeys," Kate answered.

"I want to see a scary lion with a loud roar," said Tom.

"Well, you're both in luck," said Uncle Mike. "We can see all those and more!"

beautiful

scary

silly

Adjectives help create a clear picture for readers and listeners to imagine.

Tom and Kate used **adjectives** to tell about things they saw or wanted to see. Adjectives are words that help us learn more about **nouns**. They can be used to **describe** what color something is or how a person is feeling. They can explain how something sounds, smells, tastes, or feels. They can give details about people, places, or even ideas. If a word describes something, it is probably an adjective.

Extra Examples

Here are some common types of adjectives:

Adjectives that end in -y: happy, tasty
Adjectives that end in *-ous*: fabulous, famous
Adjectives that end in *-less*: mindless, helpless
Adjectives that end in *-able*: adorable, available
Adjectives that end in *-ful*: painful, helpful

There are many other kinds of adjectives as well.
Keep an eye out for them!

Keep an eye out for these endings. They can help you tell when a word is an adjective.

-y
-ous
-less
-ful -able

This long, green snake found a quiet spot at the busy zoo.

"Where do you want to go first?" Uncle Mike asked. He looked down at a map of the zoo.

"Let's go to the reptile house," Kate replied. "I want to see some dangerous snakes." Adjectives often come right before a noun.

"Can we go somewhere else first?" asked Tom. "Snakes are scary!" Other times, the adjective comes later in the sentence.

To get a copy of this activity, visit
www.cherrylakepublishing.com/activities.

ACTIVITY

Locate and List!

Locate and list all the adjectives in the following sentences:

"OK," said Kate. "I don't mind if we go somewhere else first."

"How about we take this long path?" asked Uncle Mike. "It will let us see big cats and some other interesting animals."

"Yeah!" said Tom. "I can't wait to see the tigers. I love their orange stripes!" Kate, Tom, and Uncle Mike walked along the paved path. They stopped to look at different animals along the way.

"Look at that furry bear," said Tom. "He sure is big!"

"That dog's fur is covered in weird spots," said Kate. She pointed at an animal in the next area.

"That is so cool!" Tom replied.

Answers: long, big, interesting, orange, paved, different, furry, big, weird, next, cool

STOP!
DON'T WRITE
IN THE BOOK!

CHAPTER TWO

Comparing Things

Kate, Tom, and Uncle Mike decided to see the elephants next. "I bet the elephants will be even cooler than the lions," Tom said. Adjectives can be used to compare different things. Adjectives comparing two things often end in *-er*.

Kate's eyes widened as they got close to the elephants. "That elephant is the biggest animal I've ever seen!" she said. Adjectives that compare more than two things often end in *-est*.

"It's more boring than the tigers, though," Tom said with disappointment. "All it does is stand there."

"I think the bears were the most boring," said Kate. "They were all sleeping." The words *more* or *most* are sometimes needed with certain adjectives to compare things.

Extra Examples

Here are some examples of adjectives that compare two or more things.

Regular	To Compare	To Show the Most
big	bigger	biggest
boring	more boring	most boring
pretty	prettier	prettiest
happy	happier	happiest
careful	more careful	most careful
important	more important	most important

Do you notice a pattern? Most adjectives with more than one **syllable** require *more* or *most* to make comparisons. Be careful, though. The rule isn't always true! For example, look at *pretty* in the chart. It has two syllables (pret-ty). But it does not use *more* or *most*. As you read books and practice writing, you will learn more about which adjectives need *more* and *most*.

"I thought the cats smelled bad," Kate said. "The elephants smelled worse," Tom replied. Some adjectives are unusual. They do not follow the normal rules of making comparisons. *Bad* changes to *worse* when it is used to make a comparison. The two words are completely different!

"Uncle Mike, that elephant's leg is as tall as you!" said Kate. Adjectives can also be used to describe the way two things are similar. To do this, *as* is placed before and after the adjective.

Locate and List!

Locate and list all the adjectives that compare things in the following sentences. Be sure to only list an adjective if it is comparing things!

"Let's go look at some animals that are funnier than elephants," said Tom.

"Monkeys are the funniest animals of all," said Kate.

"The monkey house is this way," said Uncle Mike. "Let's go." Tom and Kate followed their uncle along a short path. They all went into the monkey house.

"Look at the one with the long tail," said Kate. "The way it moves is so silly!"

"The little brown one is even sillier than the long-tailed one," said Tom. "Look how far it can jump!"

"It can jump far," agreed Kate. "But it can't jump as far as that tiny gray one with the colorful face!"

Answers: funnier, funniest, sillier, as far as

To get a copy of this activity, visit www.cherrylakepublishing.com/activities.

CHAPTER THREE

Other Types of Adjectives

This monkey is particularly fast!

"The tiny monkey with the fuzzy face is so fast," said Tom. He watched the monkey zip across a log and climb up a tree.

"A monkey that fast would be really hard to catch," Kate added.

"An elephant could never move that fast," Tom said.

Small words like *the*, *a*, and *an* tell us about nouns, too. In some cases, these words are adjectives. For example, in the first sentence, Tom talked about one specific monkey. Words like *a* and *an* are less specific. When Kate says "a monkey," she was not talking about one specific monkey. She was talking about any monkey.

The phrase "a lion" could refer to any lion.

To get a copy of this activity, visit
www.cherrylakepublishing.com/activities.

ACTIVITY

Read and Rethink

Read the following passage. Then rewrite it and fill in the correct word, choosing from *the*, *a*, and *an*:

Tom, Kate, and Uncle Mike decided to visit _____ birds next. "I can't wait to see _____ parrot," Kate said as they walked toward _____ bird area.

"One time Dad showed me _____ eagle in the backyard," Tom said. "That is _____ coolest bird I've ever seen."

"Wait until you see _____ birds here," said Uncle Mike. "They are all colors, sizes, and shapes."

Answer:

Tom, Kate, and Uncle Mike decided to visit **the** birds next. "I can't wait to see **a** parrot," Kate said as they walked toward **the** bird area.

"One time Dad showed me **an** eagle in the backyard," Tom said. "That is **the** coolest bird I've ever seen."

"Wait until you see **the** birds here," said Uncle Mike. "They are all colors, sizes, and shapes."

Tom and Kate didn't know where to look first as they walked into the bird area. Inside a giant net, birds of all sizes and colors flew overhead from tree to tree. "Hey, look," said Tom. "That one is the same color as Kate's shirt!" Adjectives can describe who owns, or **possesses**, something.

"There must be 100 birds in here," said Kate. Her eyes darted from one bird to the next. Numbers are also used as adjectives. They describe how many of something there are.

Adjectives can show how many of something there are.

"We'd better move along," said Uncle Mike. "It's getting late, and we still have to go to the reptile house."

"Alright!" shouted Kate. "I'm ready to see some snake teeth." Nouns can often be used as adjectives. *Reptile* and *snake* are both nouns, but they can also be used to describe other nouns.

Tom covered his eyes as they walked through the door of the reptile house.

"Whoa!" said Kate as she ran toward the biggest snake in sight. "Look at that one!"

"Which snake is your favorite?" Kate asked Tom, who was still covering his eyes.

Extra Examples

There are three common types of pronouns that can be used as adjectives:

Those that show who or what something belongs to: my, mine, your, yours, her, hers, his, its, their, theirs
Those that tell us which thing is being discussed: that, this, those, these
Those that ask questions: which, what, whose

"None of them," answered Tom. "Let's go somewhere else now!"

Pronouns are words that replace nouns, such as *he*, *she*, *that*, *this*, or *it*. Sometimes pronouns act as adjectives. Pronouns that show who possesses something are adjectives, such as *his* in "his eyes." So are pronouns that show which part of a group is being talked about, such as *that* in "that one." *Which* and other question pronouns are also adjectives.

Whenever you describe something, you use adjectives.

"We'd better get ready to go," said Uncle Mike as he looked at his watch. "The zoo is closing soon. Did you see everything you wanted to see?"

"Yeah, all the animals we saw were amazing!" said Kate.

"Except for those yucky reptiles!" added Tom.

ACTIVITY

Read and Rethink!

Read the following sentences. Then rewrite them, filling in the blanks with adjectives you think will work:

Uncle Mike took Tom and Kate to the _____ shop on the way out of the zoo. "You can each pick out _____ thing," he said. Tom and Kate looked at all of the _____ stuff in the store.
    "I like _____ one," said Tom as he held up a _____ figure of a lion. "But it's not as _____ as this one," he added, picking up a _____ figure. "_____ one are you getting, Kate?"
    "_____ shirt is _____ ," said Kate. "But I think I want this _____ hat." Uncle Mike paid for the gifts, and they walked outside toward the _____ lot.
    "Thanks so much, Uncle Mike," said Kate.
    "Yeah," Tom added, "this was the _____ day ever!"

To get a copy of this activity, visit www.cherrylakepublishing.com/activities.

Glossary

adjectives (AJ-ik-tivz) words that describe nouns or pronouns

describe (di-SKRIBE) to tell about something

details (DEE-taylz) small pieces of information

nouns (NOWNZ) words that represent objects, people, places, animals, or ideas

possesses (poh-ZESS-iz) owns or holds

pronouns (PRO-nownz) words that replace a noun or a noun phrase

syllable (SIL-uh-buhl) chunks of a word that can be said in one beat. For example, *love* has one beat, and *happy* has two.

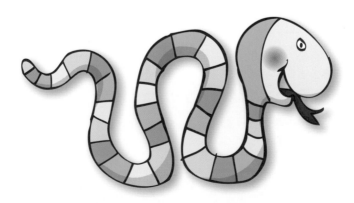

For More Information

BOOKS

Dahl, Michael. *If You Were an Adjective*. Minneapolis: Picture Window Books, 2006.

Fisher, Doris, and D. L. Gibbs. *Bowling Alley Adjectives*. Pleasantville, NY: Gareth Stevens, 2008.

WEB SITE

Between the Lions—The Best Trampolini Game
http://pbskids.org/lions/games/trampolini.html
Play a game to test your adjective knowledge!

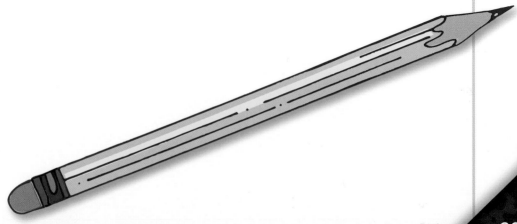

Index

-*able* endings, 7

common types, 7, 19
comparisons, 10, 11, 12, 13

descriptions, 6, 12, 17, 18
details, 6

-*er* endings, 10

-*ful* endings, 7

-*less* endings, 7

nouns, 6, 8, 15, 18, 19
numbers, 17

possessive adjectives, 17, 19

pronouns, 19

questions, 19

sentences, 8, 9, 13, 16, 21
similarities, 12
specific nouns, 15, 16
syllables, 11

unusual adjectives, 12

-*y* endings, 7

About the Author

Josh Gregory writes and edits books for kids. He lives in Chicago, Illinois.